Metamorphosis Factor

Contact with Heaven–The Rehearsal
Matthew 17; Mark 9; Luke 9

Jeffrey D. Johnson

Wipf & Stock
PUBLISHERS
Eugene, Oregon

Wipf and Stock Publishers
199 W 8th Ave, Suite 3
Eugene, OR 97401

Metamorphosis Factor
Contact with Heaven--The Rehearsal: Matthew 17, Mark 9, Luke 9
By Johnson, Jeffrey D.

ISBN 13: 978-1-55635-075-7
ISBN 10: 1-55635-075-9
Publication date 11/30/2006

About Israel Today Ministries

Three-fold Purpose:

- Teach the Church about Israel
- Teach Israel about their Messiah
- Help feed those in need (Romans 15:27; Genesis 12:1-3)

To receive Dr. Johnson's "teaching letters," or, if you would like to send a gift to Israel Today Ministries, or if you would like Dr. Johnson to speak at your church event, school, or small group, contact:

Israel Today Ministries
P.O. Box 150288
Arlington, TX 76015
Phone/Fax 817.468.4441
E mail: Galileeman@juno.com

This is Yossef (Joseph) and Abigail. Your monthly donations help feed little ones like these.

"Inasmuch as ye have done it unto one of the least of these my brethren, ye have done it unto me" –Jesus, Matthew 25:40

About Dr. Jeffrey D. Johnson

- Three decades in ministry
- Founder/Director of Israel Today Ministries
- Director of tours to the Middle East
- Senior pastor in Ohio, Massachusetts and California
- Almost 7 years directorship with International Ministries to Israel (formerly, The American Association for Jewish Evangelism, where the famed Hyman Appelman was the first president)
- Conference speaker
- Bible expositor
- Guest lecturer
- Author

Born and raised in the Midwest, Dr. Johnson took his B.D. from Massillon Baptist College, his MA from Moody Bible Institute, and his Th.M. and Th.D. from Christian Bible College. His passion for Israel, the Jewish roots of Christianity and Bible prophecy, is well known. His teaching will stir your heart to follow the Lord and to love and *"pray for the peace of Jerusalem"* (Psalm 122:6).

As an "Itinerant Bible Teacher," Dr. Johnson will travel anywhere to proclaim God's redeeming Grace through our Lord and Savior Jesus the Messiah, *"to the Jew first, and also to the Greek"* (Romans 1:16).

His call is to *"Teach the Church about Israel; Teach Israel about their Messiah; and to feed those in need"* (Genesis 12:3; Romans 15:27).

Dr. Jeff and his wife, Louise, have purposed to serve the Lord trusting God to provide the funds and resources for their livelihood.

Israel Today Ministries, founded by Dr. Johnson, is a faith ministry, supported by "love offerings" from those desiring to bless Israel. Dr. Jeff and Louise have been commissioned and sent out by their home church.

Comments from Christian Leaders

I am pleased to recommend him to churches as an able expositor of the Word of God.

– *the late* **John Walvoord**, Chancellor,
Dallas Theological Seminary

A Bible Expositor with special insights on the origin, nature and destiny of God's chosen people, Israel.

– **John C. Whitcomb**, Bible Scholar, Author, Professor

A careful expositor of Scripture.

– **Homer Kent**, President Emeritus,
Grace College and Seminary

A practitioner of all that he preaches.

– **Paige Patterson**, former President of the
Southern Baptist Convention, President,
Southeastern Baptist Theological Seminary

He has a wonderful grasp of Jewish history and liturgy.

– **Edgar C. James**, Professor, Moody Bible Institute

He is a person who has been uniquely prepared by God to preach and teach about God's special people. Any one who hears him will come away with a great love for the people of Abraham.

–**Dick Dahlquist**, Chair, Pastoral Studies, Acting Dean,
Grace College of Graduate Studies

He has a gifted teaching ministry which encompasses Biblical prophecy and insights into modern-day Judaism.

–the late **Paul Tassell**, Bible Scholar, Author,
former National Representative of the G.A.R.B.C.

He has a great ministry.

– **LaVerne Butler**, former President of Mid-Continent Baptist College, Scholar, Conference Speaker, President, Pulpit Aflame

Your heart will be thrilled as he ministers the prophetic Scriptures.

– the late **Alden A. Gannett**, President Emeritus of Southeastern Bible College, Bible Scholar, Author, Conference Speaker, President, Gannett Ministries

He loves the people and nation of Israel. He has given himself to a thorough study of God's ancient people and of the prophetic.

– **Ivan H. French**, Pastor Emeritus, Pleasant View Bible Church, former Professor, Grace College and Seminary

Contact with Heaven–The Rehearsal

"And after six days Jesus taketh Peter, James and John his brother, and bringeth them up into an high mountain apart" Matthew 17:1

During the last six months of the Lord's Life on Earth between verses one and two of chapter seven a most incredible episode took place. John mentions it in chapter 1:14,

"...We (Peter, James, and John) beheld his glory, the glory as of the only begotten of the Father,) full of grace and truth."

Verse 1: *"After these things Jesus walked in Galilee: for he would not walk in Jewry, because the Jews sought to kill him."*

Because the tenses are all imperfect, a better rendering would be, "After these things Jesus was walking in Galilee, for He did not desire to walk in Judaea, because the religious rulers sought to kill Him." Please take note in verse two the Feast of the Tabernacles was at hand...

Verse 2: *"Now the Jews' feast of tabernacles was at hand."*

The incredible event was the Transfiguration.

Jesus took his three choice disciples up to Mt. Hermon to pray. Some believe this scene took place on Mt. Tabor. This is unlikely due to the fact that there was a fortress on top of Tabor during the time of Christ. Hermon is 9,400 feet high and some 11,000 feet above the Jordan Valley and can be seen from the Dead Sea, which is more than 100 miles away. This would have been a most difficult climb in which the men would not have reached the summit. More than likely they were on one of the slopes.

It was beginning to become nightfall. Some believe this was the evening after the Sabbath. The panorama from Hermon would have been glorious. They would have seen part of Syria, Lebanon, the Jordan Valley, the Dead Sea, Galilee, Samaria and Jerusalem. The stars shining brilliant in the sky. The moon would have cast shadows from the trees. Patches of glistening snow would be illuminated. Far from the religious polemic of the Scribes and Pharisees. Upon this mountain which stood between the Hebraic and Hellenistic cultural influences. Upon this mountain, Jesus prayed to His Father to verify whether this was the time for which He came.

Peter, James and John were the Lord's most trusted men. He took them with Him, not only to Mt. Hermon, but also to the house of Jairus when Jesus healed his twelve year-old daughter and to the Garden.

"And when he came into the house, he suffered no man to go in, save Peter, and James, and John, and the father and the mother of the maiden." Luke 8:51

"And it came to pass about an eight days after these sayings, he took Peter and John and James, and went up into a mountain to pray." Luke 9:28

Into a High Mountain to Pray

This reminds us of Abraham ascending to Moriah with Isaac testing their faith...Affirming the truthfulness, holiness and mercy of God as He provided the ram for sacrifice. And Moses' ascent to Sinai entering the presence of God via the burning bush...then ultimately entering the Shekinah glory, being the recipient of the Law among the thundering and light of the Creator's essence. It reminds us of Elijah receiving sustenance from an angel after a great victory on Carmel, running from Jezebel, ascending to Mt. Horeb, (the same place Moses met with God in the Sinai) hearing the still small voice of God, saying... 'Go on Elijah, I have 7,000 who have not bowed down to Baal, who have not kissed him.' Now, Jesus comes to the mountain to seek His Father's will.

After the ascent to Hermon, Luke records that Peter, James and John were heavy with sleep. (They would also fall asleep in the Garden.) This is very natural after an arduous, steep climb up a mountain path. Exhausted, perhaps battling the thin mountain air, weakened by hunger and thirst...They fall asleep only to be awakened by a most glorious sight.

"But Peter and they that were with him were heavy with sleep: and when they were awake, they saw his glory, and the two men that stood with him." Luke 9:32

"What they saw was their Master, while praying, transformed. The 'form of God' shone through the 'form of a servant': the 'appearance of His Face became other', 'it did shine as the sun'...the whole figure seemed bathed in light, the very garments whiter far than the snow on which the moon shone... 'flittering', 'white as the light'."[1]

Transfigured

"And was transfigured before them: and his face did shine as the sun, and his raiment was white as the light." Matthew 17:2

"And after six days Jesus taketh with him Peter, and James, and John, and leadeth them up into an high mountain apart by themselves: and he was transfigured before them." Mark 9:2

Greek—"metemorphothe" gives us our English word "metamorphosis." "A metamorphosis is a change on the outside that comes from the inside...Our Lord's glory was not reflected but radiated from within. There was a change on the outside that came from within as He allowed His essential glory to shine forth."[2]

"And as he prayed, the fashion of his countenance was altered, and his raiment was white and glistering." Luke 9:29

Luke tells us "his countenance was altered"...which means Jesus "became other", "different", "strange", something quite unknown. The writer of Hebrews states that

"The Son is the radiance of God's glory and the exact representation of His being." Hebrews 1:3 (NIV)

Peter, James and John were experiencing a glimpse of the very essence and glory of God the Father through God the Son. The very Shekinah glory of Sinai and the godesh ha godeshim was in their presence.

What an affirmation of Peter's confession at Caeserea Phillipi at the base of Mt. Hermon when Jesus asked His disciples… "Whom do men say that I the Son of man am?" … Peter answered and said,

"Thou art the Christ, the Son of the living God." Matthew 16:16

Peter confessed then received assurance.

Like Mary and Martha, whose brother Lazarus died. When Jesus arrived they said, "Lord, if thou hadst been here, (our brother would not have died). Jesus said,

"I am the resurrection, and the life: he that believeth in me, though he were dead, yet shall he live: And whosoever liveth and believeth in me shall never die. Believest thou this"? John 11:25,26

They believed and rolled away the stone and Jesus said, "Lazarus, come forth…loose him, and let him go!

Elijah and Moses

"And, behold, there talked with him two men, which were Moses and Elias" Luke 9:30

It was quite fitting for these two pillars of the Old Testament to appear. First of all, both Moses and Elijah had unique obituaries written about them. Deuteronomy tells of the mysterious death of Moses on Mount Nebo overlooking the Dead Sea, Jericho and the Promised Land. The Scriptures gives us the impression that God Himself buried the Great Giver of the Law. Elijah's departure in a chariot and horses of fire was nothing less than awesome as Elisha, his disciple, beheld his ascension into the heavens.

Jewish scholars teach that Moses is to accompany the Messiah and be His consort. ...And Elijah is to call the people of Israel back to God and prepare the way for, and herald the coming of, the Messiah and the Messianic Kingdom.

Moses was the greatest of the law-givers and Elijah was the greatest prophet. "These two men were the twin peaks of Israel's religious history and achievement."[3] The foundation of the Law and the pillar of the prophets. "In them all history rose up and pointed Jesus on His way. In them all history recognized Jesus as its own consummation."[4]

The Conversation

"Who appeared in glory, and spake of his decease which he should accomplish at Jerusalem." Luke 9:31

There are two Greek words translated "decease or deceased".

1. Teleutao (tel-yoo-taht-o) to decease or to end life (Matthew 22:25).
2. Exodus- out-going (Luke 9:31) Peter uses the same word referencing his own "out-going", in the context of describing the Transfiguration (2 Peter 1:15). To understand "exodus", or out-going, we must contrast Luke's antonym describing the Lord's "in-coming".

"When John had first preached before his coming the baptism of repentance to all the people of Israel" Acts 13:24

"Eisodos" (icé-od-us) - Eisodos means entrance, into, of place, time or purpose...a road or journey. Paul speaking at a synagogue in Antioch in Pisidia, gave a synopsis of the anticipation of the "in-coming" or entrance of the Messiah. He talked about the Exodus, Judges, Prophets, David's seed from which Messiah would come and John the Baptist preaching "before his eisodos" (coming)...before Messiah's purposed journey began.

Now, on Mt. Hermon, we have a dialogue concerning the Messiah's exodos, His "out-going." Ending His purposed journey...which embraces not only His death, but its method and resurrection and ascension. This "He should accomplish at Jerusalem."

Accomplish- Pleroo (play-ró-o) means to make full, fill out, to fulfill, perfect.

So the dialogue that was on the lips of Moses and Elijah was relative to Jesus fulfilling the Law, fulfilling the prophecies, types and shadows...What a holy, eternal moment these precious disciples observed. This experience became paramount for these three disciples. It was good for these men to have witnessed a glimpse of the future glory which was theirs and...is for all who trust in Christ alone.

This became a motivational impetus for them as James became the first apostle to be martyred by Herod's hand of hatred. Herod hated him because James was tenacious like the Rock of Gibraltar. Peter, the most human of the apostles, ultimately stood gloriously for Christ even unto death as he was crucified, upside down. And John, who was imprisoned, boiled in oil and exiled to Patmos and was the last apostle to die. They remembered Mt. Hermon, therefore, did not fear their "out-going", their exodus, end of their journey.

Three Tabernacles

"And it came to pass, as they departed from him, Peter said unto Jesus, Master, it is good for us to be here: and let us make three tabernacles; one for thee, and one for Moses, and one for Elias: not knowing what he said." Luke 9:33

Peter saw this event in connection with the Feast of Tabernacles, also called Feast of Booths or Succoth. Succoth is celebrated each year in the Autumn, reminding Jewish people of the Exodus, living in booths or tents (temporary dwellings) until the younger generation would be allowed to enter the Promised Land. It also looked forward to Israel's full blessings from God when He gathers His people into the land in the last days. The Feast of Tabernacles points to the Messiah's reign on earth, the Millennial Kingdom.

Mark tells us that Peter did not know what to say, because they were terrified.

"For he wist not what to say; for they were sore afraid" Mark 9:6

Peter had the right idea, but the wrong time.

The Cloud

"While he thus spake, there came a cloud, and overshadowed them: and they feared as they entered into the cloud." Luke 9:34

"A strange peculiarity has been noticed about Hermon in 'the extreme rapidity of the formation of the clouds on the summit...In a few minutes a thick cap forms over the top of the mountain, and as quickly disperses and entirely disappears.'"[5] Suddenly, this cloud appears on the brow of the mountain. A very unusual cloud. A cloud that is illuminated, full of light that "overshadowed" them.

"While he yet spake, behold, a bright cloud overshadowed them: and behold a voice out of the cloud, which said, this is my beloved Son, in whom I am well pleased; hear ye him." Matthew 17:5

"And there was a cloud that overshadowed them: and a voice came out of the cloud, saying, this is my beloved Son: hear him." Mark 9:7

"Overshadowed" means to cast a shadow upon, to envelope or enwrap in a haze of brilliancy. "As it laid itself between Jesus and the two Old Testament representatives, it parted, and presently enwrapped them."[6] This was nothing less than the very "presence of God, revealing, yet concealing—a cloud, yet luminous."[7]

Terror apprehended the disciples as the fringe and shadow of this glorious cloud touched them. This was the same cloud that permeated Israel's history. This cloud led the people during the Exodus and wilderness wanderings (Exodus 13:21,22)... and covered the Tabernacle at its completion (Exodus 40:34)...and filled the house of the Lord at the dedication of Solomon's Temple (1 Kings 8:10, 11; 2

Chronicles 5:13; 7:2). Perhaps, most memorable is when this Divine Glory, the Shekinah, came down upon Mount Sinai on the very top of the mountain. Let's read…

"And Moses brought forth the people out of the camp to meet with God; and they stood at the nether part of the mount. And mount Sinai was altogether on a smoke, because the Lord descended upon it in fire: and the smoke thereof ascended as the smoke of a furnace, and the whole mount quaked greatly." Exodus 19:17,18

In Jewish thought, when the Lord descended upon the mount, "when He began to lower His Shekinah. At this point, the mountain shook and rose to meet Him, as a servant runs to greet his master…the activity of the mountain: though inanimate, became alive."[8] The whole earth groans for the Glory of God.

"For we know that the whole creation groaneth and travaileth in pain together until now." Romans 8:22

All inanimate images and gods will bow down before Him.

"Confounded be all they that serve graven images, that boast themselves of idols: worship him, all ye gods." Psalm 97:7

A Voice

"While he yet spake, behold, a bright cloud overshadowed them: and behold a voice out of the cloud, which said, this is my beloved Son, in whom I am well pleased; hear ye him." Matthew 17:5

"Hear ye Him…"

To the Jew this cloud represented the very presence of God, the Shekinah. There was no mistake as to what was taking place and it is as though Matthew was astounded as to what he was writing as he said, "Behold"... (verses 3, 5)

"And, behold, there appeared unto them Moses and Elias talking with him." Matthew 17:3

...LOOK AT THIS, I WANT YOU TO UNDERSTAND, KNOW WHAT IS TAKING PLACE!

Behold, Moses and Elijah...Behold, the bright cloud... Behold, the voice out of the cloud...This voice was a confirmation for Jesus that this was the hour for which He came. It was also a confirmation for the disciples and for us...

He is *"...all and in all"* (Colossians 3:11)... *"...Ye are complete in Him..."* (Colossians 2:10)... *"He is before all things, and by him all things consist"* (Colossians 1:17)... He is truth... the totality of Truth (John 14:6).

"And when the disciples heard it, they fell on their face, and were sore afraid. And Jesus came and touched them, and said, Arise, and be not afraid. And when they had lifted up their eyes, they saw no man, save Jesus only."" Matthew 17: 6,7,8

As Isaiah trembled in the presence of the Lord and cried out,

"...Woe is me! For I am undone; because I am a man of unclean lips...for mine eyes have seen the King, the Lord of hosts." Isaiah 6:5

And as John will once again fall prostrate before a glorified Lord on the isle of Patmos... Peter, James and John fall "on their face and were sore afraid."

"Touched" (Greek Haptomai (hap'-tom-ahee) to hold on; fasten to; embrace; to set on fire.

Verse 8: *They saw no one but Jesus...*

Who do you see? Who do you look upon? CHRIST IS ALL WE NEED...

John made reference to the transfiguration when he stated,

"And the Word was made flesh, and dwelt among us (and we beheld His glory, the glory as of the only begotten of the Father), full of grace and truth." John 1:14

And Peter recalls his experience on the Mount of Transfiguration where he saw the Lord unveiled in glory. This same glory that will be seen at His coming.

"Knowing that shortly I must put off this my tabernacle, even as our Lord Jesus Christ hath shewed me. Moreover I will endeavour that ye may be able after my decease to have these things always in remembrance. For we have not followed cunningly devised fables, when we made known unto you the power and coming of our Lord Jesus Christ, but were eyewitnesses of his majesty. For he received from God the Father honour and glory, when there came such a voice to him from the excellent glory, This is my beloved Son, in whom I am well pleased. And this voice which came from heaven we heard, when we were with him in the holy mount." 2 Peter 1:14-18

"In Christ's transfiguration the disciples received a foretaste of what His coming will be like when He returns to establish His eternal kingdom." NIV study notes, 2 Peter 1:16. This was a "rehearsal" of the Second Coming. There should be no chapter division between Matthew 16:28 and 17:1.

After six days-

"And the glory of the Lord abode upon mount Sinai, and the cloud covered it six days: and the seventh day he called unto Moses out of the midst of the cloud. And the sight of the glory of the Lord was like devouring fire on the top of the mount in the eyes of the children of Israel. And Moses went into the midst of the cloud, and gat him up into the mount: and Moses was in the mount forty days and forty nights." Exodus 24:16-18

"It appears that these six days hark back to Exodus 24:16-18 and are intended to parallel the theophany at Sinai."[9]

"For the Son of man shall come in the glory of His Father, with His angels..." Matthew 16:27

"...the Son of man shall come in His glory, and all the holy angels with Him, then shall He sit upon the throne of His glory, and before Him shall be gathered all nations..." Matthew 25:31,32

"Looking for that blessed hope, and the glorious appearing of the great God and our Saviour Jesus Christ." Titus 2:13

"Behold, He cometh with clouds; and every eye shall see Him..." Revelation 1:7

John warns us, *"And now, little children, abide in Him; that, when He shall appear, we may have confidence, and not be ashamed before Him at His coming." 1 John 2:28*

Verse 9: They came down from the mountain

From here Jesus begins to conclude His public ministry heading toward the cross, the grave and resurrection Sunday.

What conclusions can we draw from this transfiguration experience?

1. **"Jesus laid aside His glory when He came to earth. Because of the finished work on the cross He not only received back His glory, but now shares it with us who believe."[10]**

"And now, O Father, glorify thou me with thine own self with the glory which I had with thee before the world was." John 17:5
"And the glory which thou gavest me I have given them; that they may be one, even as we are one: John 17:22

"Father, I will that they also, whom thou hast given me, be with me where I am; that they may behold my glory, which thou hast given me: for thou lovedst me before the foundation of the world." John 17:24

2. **We need not fear the future nor the mystery of death.**

   "There is a most comforting lesson for us in the fact that the disciples knew Moses and Elijah. We will not have to be introduced when we get to heaven but '…

then shall I know even as also I am known' (1 Corinthians 13:12). Likewise, the heavenly visitors knew what was transpiring on earth and of the coming crucifixion of the Saviour... Our loved ones who have gone on before know what is transpiring on earth. They cannot speak to us but they are a great cloud of witnesses about us (Hebrews 12:1). They rejoice in the presence of the angels when a sinner repents.

"I say unto you, that likewise joy shall be in heaven over one sinner that repenteth, more than over ninety and nine just persons, which need no repentance." Luke 15:7

"Likewise, I say unto you, there is joy in the presence of the angels of God over one sinner that repenteth." Luke 15:10

The unseen world is not far away and how happy are they who are with the Saviour there."[11]

3. **Because of this "rehearsal" or glimpse of our future glory we have hope.**

"Behold, what manner of love the Father hath bestowed upon us, that we should be called the sons of God: therefore the world knoweth us not, because it knew him not. Beloved, now are we the sons of God, and it doth not yet appear what we shall be: but we know that, when he shall appear, we shall be like him; for we shall see him as he is. And every man that hath this hope in him purifieth himself, even as he is pure." 1 John 1:1-3

John was there...Rejoice, beloved, rejoice...In the hope of eternal glory that is ours for those in Christ. Do you see Christ only? Do you see Him?

Endnotes

[1] Alfred Edersheim, *"The Life and Times of Jesus the Messiah,"* (Longmans, Green, and Co.), New York, 1910), p. 96.
[2] Warren W. Wiersbe, *"Be Loyal"*, (Victor Books, Wheaton, 1980), p. 117.
[3] William Barclay, *"The Gospel of Matthew, Volume 2"*, (The Westminster Press, Philadelphia, 1958), p. 176.
[4] Ibid., p. 177.
[5] Alfred Edersheim, *"The Life and Times of Jesus, The Messiah"*, (Longmans, Green, and Co., New York, 1910), p. 97.
[6] Ibid., p. 97.
[7] Ibid., p. 97.
[8] S.Y. Agnon, *"Present at Sinai, The Giving of the Law"*,(The Jewish Publication Society, Philadelphia-Jerusalem, 5754-1994), p. 186.
[9] Samuel Tobres Lach, *"A Rabbinic Commentary on the New Testament"*, (KTAV Publishing House, New Jersey, 1987), p. 259.
[10] Warren W, Wiersbe, *"Be Loyal"*, (Victor Books, Wheaton, 1980), p. 117.
[11] John R. Rice, *"The King of the Jews", A Verse-by-Verse Commentary, Matthew,* (Sword of the Lord Publishers, Murfreesboro, Tennessee, 1955), pp. 260-261.